FOR

Although we are a nation of poets we are accused of not reading poetry, or buying poetry books. After many years of listening to the incessant gripes of poetry publishers, I can only assume that the books they publish, in general, are books that most people do not want to read.

Poetry should not be obscure, introverted, and as cryptic as a crossword puzzle: it is the poet's duty to reach out and embrace the world.

The world owes the poet nothing and we should not be expected to dig and delve into a rambling discourse searching for some inner meaning.

The reason we write poetry (and almost all of us do) is because we want to communicate: an ideal; an idea; or a specific feeling. Poetry is as essential in communication, as a letter; a radio; a telephone, and the main criterion for selecting the poems in this anthology is very simple: they communicate.

A HINT OF SUNSHINE

Edited by

Kelly Oliver

First published in Great Britain in 2002 by
POETRY NOW
Remus House,
Coltsfoot Drive,
Peterborough, PE2 9JX
Telephone (01733) 898101
Fax (01733) 313524

HB ISBN 0 75432 828 7
SB ISBN 0 75432 829 5

CONTENTS

SEAVIEW

Pebbles and sand, driftwood on land,
a view of the sea, a strange garden, no green lawn,
no flowers, maybe a tree.
Wild grass trying to grow in a patch of sand.
No formal garden is to be found, not here on
Seaview ground.
The old house painted a faded green; it has a look of age
and wear, but loved none the less.
Never forgotten, always there for when the family visit.
Loved, remembered, happy days shared, children grown
but Seaview is still there.

Joyce B Burton

SEPTEMBER

The beauty of the summer's thrown away.
September lights chrysanthemums.
Children kick the falling leaves,
And I, when I find all of autumn's poems,
Will have laughed my hair to rain,
New candles burning in my heart.

Marion Schoeberlein

EASTER

We are looking forward
At this time for spring
To come along
With anticipation
We watch the signs
And hear the skylarks sing
The days are growing longer
There are buds upon the tree
A promise of good times to come
And beautiful flowers to see
This new awakening of the Earth
Epitomising a gigantic birth

Mary Tickle

DEATH OF A TREE

It fell, one night of gale,
my proud, tall standing tree
defenceless on the ground,
sad agony.

Gashed, maimed and broken,
tears oozing from the bark,
cleft gashes showing
its inner heart.

I cried for this tree of mine
for life so quickly gone,
for its tender beauty and grace
and whispering song.

But look, spring has come,
strong shoot of tender green
grows from the ancient stump
child of my tree.

Margaret Renshaw

HURRAH FOR SUMMER

Summer sun is here again,
Warming rays that melt the cold.
Seeing happy, smiling faces
Of the people, young and old.
Jack Frost safely tucked away
And the snow has vanished.
Looking forward to sunny days,
Tears and sorrow banished.
That's what sunny days are for.
Loads of laughter, having fun.
Time for meeting friends, and then
Relaxing in the warming sun.

E Timmins

ROSE

Unfurling, revealing your innermost part,
From a tightly held bud you disclose your heart.
Seductively opening your petals to show
Your beauty, in full bloom, a glorious rose.
Now, poised and graceful, your deep red face
Enriches the garden for eyes to embrace.

Softly the wind whispers round your stem,
Your garments cascade to be captured again
By the warm summer lawn, where you lie in the dusk
Perfuming the air with your sweet fragrant musk.

June Cooper

BY STREAM AND GLADE

Walk softly as a summer breeze by yonder stream
feel the warmth of nature's love upon your face,
Listen to the gift of song by a choir on the wing
let your heart dance to joyful sounds above.

Settle yourself in a flowery glade to dream
of your love who comes drifting through leaves of lace,
There as nature in full voice to you does sing
hold this moment in your soul, for this is nature's love.

John Clarke

DAFFODILS

Daffodilia
Daffodelusions
Daffodelerium
Daffodils
Daffodils sprouting up everywhere
in roundabouts, gardens, parks, by rivers, under bridges, on forest paths
Daffodiffusion
Yellow daffodelicacy
Daffodelicious to see
I succumb to the unique
daffodelivery of spring
in wild daffodementia
Happy yellow flower
laughing effortlessly
amidst all the green, under clouds, in wind, in rain . . .
Pure daffodelight.

Mary Pampolini-Roberts

PATHETIC FALLACY

I wept, but an iron-hued sky no drop did shed,
My friends were cold, the wind was yet more chill,
Mourned, but cerulean heavens smiled overhead,
Joyed, and they with rain threatening clouds did fill.
When disaster, like lightning struck my inner being
And a storm was raging there as never before
Nature was calm and gentle, all serene,
And did no longer blast as heretofore.

Nature I love - but to be calmed or consoled
On her alone I never will depend,
For, before God's throne, in His word I am told,
There stands a faithful, sympathetic friend.
On Earth He suffered hunger, thirst and weakness,
Our mind's distress and body's pain He knows,
He understands our sorrows and our weariness
And how it feels to be beset by foes.

And because He knew that sin was root and stem
Of all our troubles, bravely His face He set
Like a flint to go outside Jerusalem
Where on Calvary all the hordes of hell He met
And conquered! Now in heaven above
His sympathy remains, no fallacy,
As He prays for all the objects of His love.
Turn from your sin and trust Him. Then you'll see.

V M Archer

QUIET RAPTURE

Beside the cottage in the sun,
The sound wind murmurs of summer to come.
When light and sunshine is warm and kind
And all the flowers stand on parade,
With their colours on display,
To captivate your mind and heart.
My gaze would linger in this quiet rapture,
That fills my eyes with this beauty so fair,
Like the sweet flowers no one can compare.

Elisabeth Dill Perrin

SPRING FEVER

In May, a poet's moods and whims,
Drive him to sing out springtime hymns:
'The air is mild, the skies so blue,
Let me declare my love for you!
Your lips are ruddier than the cherry,
Let's join young lambs in making merry!'

But something's wrong on this May morn -
The world looks dreary and forlorn.
Instead of sweet spring's sunny glow,
An unexpected fall of snow.
Although my heart so full of love is,
I'm wearing my warm winter woollies!

Alan Swift

A Renewal

Spirit power will shower
Its blessings in nature's dressing,
Distilling juice and scent
For the arrival of Lent.

When the winter months are fled
A green carpet will be spread
And glad tidings will come
With the advent of the sun.

M MacDonald-Murray

STAGNANT WATERS

Like a stagnant pool my rhymes lie deep,
Nothing in my slumber stirs.
No beauty lures me from my sleep,
My inspiration's choked with burrs.
Oh! For the wind of joyous thought
To move the sluggish stream,
To make me pen the things I ought,
Arouse me from this dream.
Around the land sweet spring awakes,
Imbues with life the dormant earth.
All nature of her gift partakes . . .
Why then for me no bubbling mirth?
Perhaps my muse has hence decreed
That words should cease their flow.
As bubbles trapped in cloying weed
They've vanished with the undertow.

Evelyn Balmain

AFTER CHRISTMAS

This 'after Christmas' season,
The season of depression!
Rain and wind, the new invention,
Then the floods, create more tension.

Move the cattle to high ground,
Move the trees, that have fallen down.
Tow them from the roads and towns
Till once again normal life abounds.

But, will it last or will it snow?
In about two months we just might know
We listen to 'forecasts' every day,
Is it reliable what they say?

Weather whatever the season!
It only stands to reason -
Some will be good, some will be bad
But with three months gone - now we are glad!

Cindy White

CHERRY TREE

Morning creeps a smile
Making peace of early summer,
In this bright pride to celebrate
The cherry tree shows its delight.

It is such a beautiful sight
With all its pink and white petals,
Capturing the silver sky, on the natural flow,
Gathering sweet perfumes.

There is a bird, heaven high
Singing sweet nothings, which fills the air,
Listen to fluting notes,
Miracle leads through embracing culture.

There to enjoy the fresh occasion
Bright beginnings around the garland world,
All this sunlight ringing out the warm horizon
Because the cherry tree stands in full glory.

Heather Aspinall

TAKING STOCK

Days are becoming longer - it's light when I arise,
I plan the day inside my head - full of lows and highs.
Venture in the garden, bulbs are surfacing once again,
All the shrubs are now in leaf, benefiting from the rain.
I long to view the daffodils, so slender and so tall,
The beauty of the tulips and the crocuses so small.
And there will be the roses and hollyhocks in June,
Another birthday popping up (which really is too soon!)
The summer to look forward to, walks along the shore,
Coaches down from London, exciting faces and so much more . . .
To see day-trippers on the prom, enjoying sea front fairs,
Shedding daily chores and things - the worries and the cares.
For me, there is the country, essential picnics, and the walks,
Butterflies and birds to watch for, which Bill Oddie spoke of,
                                        in his talks.
Meeting up with friends again, my swans, the sheep and lambs,
Grandchildren playing with water and devising boats and dams.
Hanging out the washing - no need to worry - 'Will it rain?'
(As I go on my travels, till I get home again.)
So much to see in Sussex, there are castles and the downs,
Busy, bustling Brighton, the 'lanes' to spend those pounds!
Chances to do so many things, never done before,
Places to visit, history to learn - opening up some doors-
For me to take up hobbies, to re-evaluate my mind -
To promise myself I'll do more things, if I can only find the time!
To do more in my garden, and not to watch the clock,
It's all down to re-assessment , and fully taking stock!

Iris Cone

SPRING INTO SUMMER

The complete and utter pleasure
of a bright, warm April day
the sky as blue as cornflowers
heralds summer's on its way
New lambs start their bleating
and plants clamour for the sun
their buds are fit to bursting
as they open one by one
The birds collect in clusters
to pick this year's new mate
and start the job of nesting
before it gets too late
There's a new refreshing promise
of a life that's full again
as the sun warms up the earth
after all last winter's rain

So here we are again Lord
at the dawning of the spring
waiting to see the wonders
that your love will bring

D E Cornell

AS HE PASSES AWAY

She stands adorned in purest white,
Crisp folds of frost around her form.
A rosy blush upon her cheeks
The sun's cast as a new day's born.

A veil of mist conceals her eyes,
Crystal droplets bedeck her hair,
Snowdrops hang as glistening pearls:
Never before was spring so fair!

The age-old apple tree sheds down
Its confetti petals of pink,
New life begins from where they fell
To continually forge the link.

Bird's have borrowed a nesting bough
And music is piped by the leaves,
Bluebells line the path to the aisle
As, through the air, she softly weaves.

Bridesmaids dance in daffodil gowns,
Fairy-rings, through the grass, stand proud.
Tulips chime the approaching hour
When winter's head, at last, is bowed.

Heaven and Earth will pass away,
Mortal emotions will be numb,
Prepare to drink a rev'rent toast:
The Spirit and the Bride say, 'Come!'

Love's legacy of life reveals
A beauty there's no denying,
Creator awaits created,
To have and to hold: undying.

Wendy R Thomas

EASTER

A   very emotional time of year

W   hen we think of our dear Lord
O   f how he was nailed upon a cross
O   f how he suffered a Roman's sword
D   eath he bore with dignity
E   ven forgave his enemies
N   o greater love had man

C   rucified, he died for you and me
R   ejoice that you have known such love
O   ver these Easter days
S   ing a song of gratitude
S   ing a song of praise.

Violet M Corlett

SPRING AWAKES

Winter days give way to spring
Winter nights are on the wing
Longer days, shorter nights
Budding, bursting, spring delights

Fading time of idle leisure
Goodbye days of winter pleasure
And with early springtime yawns
Comes the threat of work on lawns

Scarifying to kill the moss
Making up the winter loss
Well-fed grass fastly growing
Long hours spent on edging, mowing

Trimming, sweeping, planting borders
Meeting all those wifely orders
Buying all those bedding plants
Preparing for a floral dance

And so the garden's at its best
Now the time for gardener's rest
Borders good, well-trimmed lawn
Fences mended, fire logs sawn

Work now done, completed all
Listening to the bench's call
And then there comes the springtime rain
And all that grass just grows again

Ray Ryan

DARK EVENINGS

Each autumn
I think I die a little!
Leaf fall and darkness
fade the colour from the scene.
Depression descends.
Endlessly long evenings
curtains drawn, world shut out,
underlines one's alone-ness.
Better settle for a book!
Or retrieve some neglected task
from obscurity and experience
a quiet satisfaction . . .
or maybe phone a friend
in need of human contact
and thereby come alive -
to others' needs, not mine alone.

Muriel E Critoph

SPRING

A glistening sheet of dew covers a garden of sullen grass.
A tightly closed bud bursts its case into bloom.
Rays of golden sunlight bounce off the rooftops.
A musical treat of a bird's wake-up call.

A gentle breeze blows through bunches of trumpet daffodils.
A silky touch delights the hand to a stroke of an animal's coat.
Children play gaily through pools of water.
The first spring raindrop falling to the ground.

Faye Conroy

THE PROMISE OF SPRING

When is it coming
And what will it bring
Is it finally here yet
The promise of spring

How long is it here for
The magpie does sing
He is singing his new song
The promise of spring

When will it be here
When will it begin
Alas, it is here
It's the promise of spring

Lyndsey Cubis

ONE DAY IN THE MONTH OF MAY

In the sun, on my sun bed, one afternoon in late May,
I listen to the sounds around, whilst in comfort I lay.
The faraway drone of the mad motorway rush,
Is in complete contrast to the trill of the thrush.

Our neighbours are gardening, busy pulling out the weeds,
The digging of the spade, which a tidy garden needs.
Further over is a lawnmower, striping up a lawn,
But it doesn't spoil the blackbird's song, as the grass is neatly mown.

Then I open one eye and peep up at the sky,
To see the sapphire blue of a ceiling so high.
It is splotched with white splashes, all abstract and bright,
And I watch, as they so slowly, move o'er the great height.

Nearer comes an aeroplane, so noisy and loud,
And as it journeys into yonder, the birds continue singing proud.
I sit up now, to view my own dear garden there,
Where smiling pansy faces are trying not to stare.

Pink, blue and purple colours cascading over the wall,
Tulips, tall and straight, above the stone crop short and small.
Bluebells guard the Oxalis, which will bloom in June/July,
While the miniature Azalea flowers, are sadly due to die.

Hebes and conifers, each different in shape and size,
Amongst Berberis and Spireas, are a varied and mingled prize.
Soon it all will change again, new life is yet to grow,
Yes, even when the sun has gone, there's life beneath the snow.

But this warm day in the month of May, is a blessing from above,
And I can feel the peace and delight of my own little world of love.
Even the gnomes look happy, and ready for the summer ahead,
And now I'm relaxed and refreshed, I can tackle my next flower bed.

Pauline Mole

THE SEASONS

Spring is the time for growing up,
Blossom, buds and birds appear,
Trees in leaf, the buttercup,
Life really is so dear.

Summer is time to reach the prime,
All is verdant and lush,
Sun is hot, it's now the time,
Enjoy it all, don't rush.

Autumn time for leaves to turn
From green to brown, then fall,
Light soon fades, and we must learn
And hope God hears our call.

Winter time for frost and snow,
The flowers and plants take rest,
On looking back does one know
Which season's really best!

All seasons give us pleasure,
From beginning to the end,
From birth to death treasure,
All our thanks to God we send.

Suzanne Joy Golding

MIRACLE OF NATURE

It greets you
When you wake.
The perfume
Pervading
The whole room.
Standing straight
Like soldiers
On duty.
In the bowl,
On the ledge.
Hyacinths
Pink and blue
Catch your eye,
As you pass
The window.
Miracles
Of nature
Peeping out.
Sleepy bulbs
Have woken.

Angela Pritchard

SPRING, TO ME

I start the winter on a high
Although the sun has said goodbye
Slowly it grows colder
Work prevents me from seeing daylight
Dark in the morning, dark at night
Christmas comes and goes
Spring feels so close
Still so far away
Just as I begin to despair
The sun begins to go
Easter eggs fill the shop
Flowers appear and new life is born
Daylight begins at early dawn
The sun begins to warm my heart
Spring brings a new start

Amanda Steel

THE BEST TIME OF THE YEAR

Summer is the best time of the year
Unique because people feel relaxed and sweet
Everywhere you go there is heat
So you can always enjoy an outside picnic treat.

Summer is the best time of the year
Because there seems to be no fear
In the city people are kept semi-clothed
And other parts bare
Motor racing, cricket and tennis are some of the outdoor sports
Done in summer's fresh, open air.

Summer is the best time of the year
Carefree and happy, that is what people will be
Stress-free and healthy, summer is for everybody
For summer is a way for nature to say:
'Sorry about that horrible weather the other day.'

Summer is the best time of the year
Where plants dazzlingly blossom
And some trees stay evergreen,
Where friendly politeness is everywhere
And a mild warmth fills your genes.

Summertime is where everyone is free
It's the best season for it to be!

Ali Sebastian

SPRING

Spring has come, full foliage dressed
With royal bloom, this season's best
The ice has gone, the cold has vanished
To winter's snowland, exiled, banished.

In sunshine's coat we're dressed and glad,
In flowers, birdsongs, nature's clad,
All comes to life, the pigeons too,
All creatures ready to mate and woo.

No more the damp, the colds, the chill,
Buds bursting through wherever they will,
All that's within, without, seems bright
The sky is blue and full of light.

A season of hope, let's surge anew,
Let us go out to dare and do,
All is renewed, made fresh again,
In solar splendour, after the rain.

Winter is hoary, cold and grim,
But even the old are full of vim
When they breathe in that springtime air,
Life seems so sprightly, challenging, fair.

Emmanuel Petrakis

WINTER

I walk among the trees
And the mist rises
Like ghosts of
times gone by

I put out my hand
The bark is cold and wet
But I can feel the strength
and life of the tree

My mind goes back
to summers gone
When streams
and brooks abounded

Where frogs and toads
nestled beneath,
The wild watercress
in the clear water

The pools of frog spawn
And little boys in wellies
With nets and jam jars
on a string

And fields a blaze of colour
With poppies, buttercups and daises
The woods, so cool and dark
carpeted with bluebells

I walk among the trees
And hear them whisper
Winter is here
But spring it yet to come

Joan May Wills

THOUGHTS OF LONG AGO

My thoughts go out on sunny days
To water rolling all along -
I paddle in my thoughts
As birds sing out their songs.

I think also of boats at sea
And how Jesus walked on water in his time,
Sunny days we need coolness
In the steam and water and seas - this we find.

My mind is full of sunshine
When I'm glowing deep down inside -
Summertime comes to greet us
With its sand and tides.

Beauty I find in my thoughts
For what I see I like to share -
So as my inner thoughts glow
Summertime is here.

My soul does a twirl of glee
When I see pictures of places in the sun -
For I do not go out much now
But all my thoughts still come.

Marion Staddon

SUMMER BY THE SEA

Rolling hills stretch to sea
As mist drifts away with the breeze.
Sunlight flickers through overhead cloud
Whilst we nestle beneath the trees.

The strength of the sun pushes through
Melting the cloud away.
Lovers stroll in the midday heat
The length and breadth of the bay.

Evening falls and a gentle wind
Cools down the sweltering sun.
Scented flowers proudly dance
As the day is nearly done.

Philip O'Leary

COUNTRY TIME

Beyond the stream, and hidden from view
Stands a rose, sparkling in the morning dew
But the grass will grow with a shower of rain
And the rose will be hidden, and not seen again.

Some cows are nearby, and are allowed to feed
On the meadow, so near to the pink rose indeed.
It's thorny stem, will keep all the animals at bay
Letting it grow, until it blooms into a fine array.

A cow gives birth, and it's lying on the ground.
I am hidden in the trees, and do not make a sound
But I hear dogs barking, and I worry for the calf
As it starts to move, but not quick enough by half.

Minutes later, my worries are short lived and gone,
As it gets to its feet, ten minutes from being born.
Its mother cleans it down, as both go for a walk,
Giving both some exercise, and mooing as if to talk.

The sun is warm, and all the plants look so bright.
Sunbeams bounce off the leaves, like a flash of light.
A field is being ploughed, and the birds follow behind
Waiting for easy prey, or anything else they can find.

The farmers are busy, growing food for the table
Row after row is planted, as far as they are able.
Soon they will be finished, letting nature do its job
Patience, manure and water, soon up they will bob.

A young hare runs by, being chased by a stray dog
But the hare left it far behind and hid behind a log.
The country is so clean, free from smoke and grime
Seeing wildlife, and plants grow, that is country time.

William A Laws

AWAITING SPRING ARRIVAL

I sit here writing this poem
On a cold winter's day.
Waiting for the spring to get going
So that the sun can play.

Heads of the flowers
Will begin to dance around.
The day will have longer hours
And the frost will exit the ground.

The sun on the water will reflect
All the colours of greens and reds
Of the trees and all the perfect
Flowers in their beds.

Oh I long for it to arrive
So that I can go and visit
All the places where nature does thrive
Where there is no pollution within it.

Michaela W Moore

DEAL IN JANUARY

Sea mist descends,
her fragile screen,
filled with the scent
of sea breeze,
lulling our senses
As her scent, gently sweeps over Kent.

Burning softly, the moon
lays down his candlelight,
lending his shadow, to twilight,
inside smoky starlit skies.
Lulling night, like a lullaby.
As the sea seeps into the sky

Night fishermen, line the pier,
their lanterns, lulling their fears.
As haunting visions, draw near,
Sailing high on salty, swelling breezes

Then, as with a sigh,
They're lost at sea,
and everything, is as it should be.
As waves rise and fall,
kissing the sea wall.
And the sky falls into the sea.

Shirley Kelleher

AN EARLY APRIL MORNING

The moon is but a shadow in the
Morning sky, the old moon, the
Waning moon, its place is ousted
By the risen sun that still is low
Behind the hills.
Birds are contemplating the morning
Quietly from their perches on the
Chimney pots and wires; their first
Glad song that came with dawn
Is silent. The earth is calm.
A little mist lies on the hills, that
Rises from the dew. The trees are
Burgeoning into leaf, the hedges
Raped in autumn by the hedge trimmer,
Their mangled branches just delicately
Veiled in tender green.
Oh yes, it's April, a month sacred
To the spring; and from my heart
Once more, there comes a song!

Elizabeth Anandadeva

DAFFODIL LOVERS

So oft I see the daffodils,
That Wordsworth saw beyond the hills.
Upon his inward eye I sit,
And splendour! At the wealth of it.
And soon my mind it fills,
With sprightly dancing daffodils.

So when in pensive mood like he,
His daffodils they set me free.
And dance upon my bathroom wall,
In winter, summer, spring or fall.
The air smells like it's off the sea,
To be shared in such a company.

As Wordsworth and his daffodils,
That I now see beyond the hills.
But lonely! Wordsworth be no more,
Cause inward eyes! Line hills and shore.
As we all hope your mind it fills,
To know we love your daffodils.

Geoffrey Woodhead

SHANTY TOWN SUMMER

We sit and slowly
Move our lips with blurred nothing
And stretch each brown bone
With sticky effort to stir.

Reduced to sweaty machines,
Cradling in the burning stench
Of rubbish, ignited by the haze
Of dirty hot, we stare at

Baby's hair, which crawls with briny wet,
Born of orange ashes.
Orange ashes we call the summer;
Rancid cancer, crusty in every inch of body.

Zoë Sutherland

SUMMER RAIN

There has to be rain
for rainbows to shine
Rainbows dancing in the sky
A sign to all that view
That soon the sun will shine again
Through clouds of darkest hue.
It lifts and cheers our spirits
Those softly coloured hues
Rainbows dancing in the sky
Chase away those dark, dark cloud blues.

Gladys Mary Gayler

Out Of Breath

In the summer,
when I was alive
out of breath,
running through the grass,
my muscles burning,
that sweet, sweet sweat
trickling down my neck,
reminding me
I was alive.

Katy Connell

DAFFODILS

Daffodils like fireworks shooting into a starry sky,
Fiery trails of colourful smoke,
Fly past of aircraft.
Unopened flower buds unlit green candles,
Incandescent as sparklers,
Tender petals lanterns in darkness.
Six-pointed stars of the cosmos,
Exploding their heady perfume,
Each trumpet a bowl of potpourri.
Stems are like rocket flares,
Petals erupting like volcanoes,
Frilly trumpets like Welsh schoolgirls' bonnets,
Worn for St David's Day.
Cheerful garden flowers,
Lemon yellow emblems of Wales,
Daffodils are sunshine in late winter,
Flares from the sun reaching out to burn.
Skyrockets and party poppers at celebrations,
Polished bronze sculptures,
Copper furnaces of the Industrial Revolution,
Noble golden flower which bloomed
Upon Welsh hillsides long before the dawn,
The cradle of industrialisation.
They flow like graceful streams amongst old pit
Workings, immortal as the Welsh language
They weave in living poetry.

Janet E Smith

THOUGHTS OF SPRING AND SUMMER

Snowdrops like Cupid's love darts,
Pierce through the cold, hard, ground,
When winter snow departs,
Bright daffodils are found.

Like golden sunshine beaming,
Making spring cleaning shine,
While hearts are high receiving,
A true love Valentine.

Those shy romantically,
A golden heart may buy,
Support children's charity,
Like stars do passing by.

Summer is advancing now,
Flowers are rainbow-hued,
With gently fragranced petals,
By butterflies pursued.

In shops there are thongs and things,
Romantic thoughts inspire,
Delicate as insect wings,
Seen through the sun's rich fire.

Birds in full song, bumble bees,
Walks in country places,
Strawberry fairs and cream teas,
Smiles on happy faces.

Kathleen Mary Scratchard

THE KOO-KWAKS O' MAY

Winter not yet over we already think of spring
The March hare running and a lark that's not on sing.
A far cry from clover but the snowdrop rears its head
The sign of what's to come as nature leave's its bed.

The grass is taking on the green, the plough is on the go
That briefing glimpse of sunshine and then the lambing snow
And rest the weary tempest on the back of winter's wing
For yet before it's over there will be a final fling
While just the other day I heard an old man say
That the biggest storm of winter came in May.

J M Heddle

THE SUNSHINE

There's been so little light,
Because I've had such a fright,
Now I know I need,
The sun ray's little seed.

Please bring me back brightness,
Instead of the never-ending darkness,
Put a cheery smile on my face,
Instead of the never-ending race.

Sometimes a glimmer do shine through,
To give you your due,
But then it goes again,
To be replaced by the pain.

Even a little ray of hope,
Would help me to cope,
It'd be worth so very much,
To feel its gentle touch.

My body needs warmth inside,
So the shadows out do slide,
Please give me your little ray,
That's all I can plead and say.

Susan Shaw

AUTUMN

Springtime is the time, so we are often told,
That should be most welcomed and most joyously received.
Writers have carelessly spilt gushing rivers
Of many-coloured inks,
Painters stretched and delicately daubed
Their canvasses - enough to cover half
The continents of Earth -
With glorification of spring; immature, unfolding spring,
Welcome after the glum, moist skies of dismal winter.
(Winter, best not thought or talked about,
Lest sadness and gloom perpetually weigh us down).
Summer, season of a million, expectant, disappointed dreams,
Of balmy days of youth, but which maybe were never real.
Summer; too wet, too hot, too dry,
A coarse disillusion,
Bemoaned by cricketers, bewailed by gardeners,
Lamented by eager tennis crowds
Who lose their passionate time
To warbling, antique stars.
Oh, Sir Cliff, although some scoff,
You're of those youthful dreams which, maybe, never were.
But Autumn, that's the time
When juicy richness bears its fruit,
Nature swells in completeness,
And shows itself mature, sweet smelling,
Perfection, glowing ready all around
Given to please all human senses,
To satisfy our eager cravings and our dreams.
We cannot savour autumn
Until we ourselves know autumn in our lives.

Arthur W Gilliland

APRIL

Here is April, here at last. This wondrous month, none can surpass.
Little lambs, happy bleating. Scented blossoms - so fleeting.
Treasure her now - too soon she'll pass.
Here is April, sunbeam filled, drip-drop little showers won't linger.
White fluffy clouds and gilly flowers - all touched by the
rainbow's finger.
Fresh breezes kiss the shimmering rills. Small creatures, still yet tender.
Those heartfelt joys shall rule my soul and I shall sing their splendour.

Here is April here at last. My own pet lamb to hold.
May God and I and angels' wings her precious life, enfold.
The laughter on her lovely face - sweet music to my heart.
With eyes, deep like the minnow pools - her smile lights up my dark.

April is as April snow. A flighty lark - a golden glow.
I wish for her the Lord to bless and comfort her in times of stress
And should she trip or stumble as she'll pass life's many themes.
May she prance and dance and soar and fly to where she'll find
her dreams.

April is as April love. A gift to us from Heaven above.
Her being I treasure - my love knows no measure.
God send peace on the wings of a dove.
May her life be lived at the rainbow's end.
Be it gold of bright-coloured hue.
Carefully take the chance - always join the dance.
Gather springtimes her whole life through.

On that April 1st morn, when she was born
I thanked God and the month that brought her.
My own, my world, my precious girl April -
My beautiful daughter.

Elizabeth Joyce Walker

A MAN'S FANCY

A man's fancy in spring is
To answer the call of nature
And find a mate if single
If not he feels a failure.

Reproduction and love
Are his only thought.
He will never rest
Till true love he has caught.

When he at last finds her
And nature's call is answered
Perhaps a baby on the way
He gives her his word.

Marriage is very hard work
Bills to pay, magic to make, loads of fun
But people should try harder
To understand how to love just one.

H G Griffiths

SNOWDROP

A herald they call me,
a harbinger of spring.
Weak, tepid sunshine
teases me from my bed.
Hope for the future, I am.

Not for me the garish colours of summer -
Orange, red or purple.
More discrete my choice
of classic cool green
and pristine white.

Allow the rest to be fussed over and cut.
I arrive when all prefer to be snug inside.
A beacon to survival I stand.
Frozen earth, carpets of snow,
will not deter me from delivering my message.
A promise of longer, lighter days
and shorter warmer nights.

Tree

SUMMER DELIGHTS

As I walked home one summer's night
I saw a silver bird on high
Against a sky of azure blue,
It left a trail of snowy white.
It was coloured by a setting sun,
Beyond the hills of Battelstead that glowing
                           sun was brilliant red.
The sun then lost its brilliant glow,
Dark clouds cast shadows on the ground below
And from the west that night drew close
To play its act of nightly host.

Now comes the dawn and with it light,
Tempts us all with more delights.
So welcome to another day,
Now Mother Nature has her part to play.
Birds, flowers, buzzing bees,
Fish, animals and trees.
Without all these our world would be,
A sombre place for you and me.

Eleanor Margaret Brooks

HOW I GET MY HIGH

It was such a beautiful morning; the sun was shining so bright.
When we opened up the curtains, the room it filled up with light.
The frost was cold and hard, there was ice all over the pond.
The garden was all white, and also in the fields beyond.
I could hear the alarm call of a blackbird, on this cold winter's day.
There must have been cats on the prowl, keen to find some prey.
The birds were queuing for the feeder; they seem to like our seed.
There is also bacon rind and fat balls; this was their hour of need.
From upstairs I can see across the fields, and the treeline up above.
There are some pigeons on the rooftops, or maybe collared doves?
Also smoke coming from the chimneys, as people light their fires.
The starlings all swooping around again, and then settling on
                                                    telephone wires.
I long to see the first crocus or snowdrop, when they burst into flower.
Then life will start to move again, and the sun will regain its power.
I want to get up every morning, and see daylight fill the sky.
Then watch nature hard at work again, that's how I get my high.

Ken Mills

SPRING IS COMING

You're certain spring will come again?
'Because it always has,' you say.
Suppose the world went wrong, and then
The seasons all just went astray?

If winter lasted all the year,
There'd be no flowers, nor fruit, nor crop.
We'd have to live from tins, I fear,
Until at last, supplies would stop.

There'd be no leaves upon the trees,
And wildlife creatures all would die.
There'd be no butterflies, nor bees,
And all the growth would be awry.

The only things that wouldn't care
Would be the creatures at the Pole.
The penguin and the polar bear
Would multiply and take their toll.

Eventu'lly, we'd have to take
Some penguin soup to stay alive.
(Or polar bear makes juicy steak)
At least, the Eskimos would thrive!

What countless summer jobs we'd lose
(No sunning by the sea I fear)
So pray the Lord will not refuse
To spring the Spring on us next year!

Alan R Wilson

SPRING

Spring is so exciting
it cannot come too soon,
I feel I can do anything
like jumping to the moon.

Nothing's insurmountable
and challenges I seek,
I simply burst with energy
as if I am a freak

Spring, two-thousand-and-two
I know will be a bust.
I can take on just anything
and also feel I must.

This spring I'm prophetic
this is the year for me.
I'll write something special
for everyone to see.

I feel optimistic
I can do anything.
If I ever become famous
it will be in the spring.

James Kimber

CORNISH WEATHER

Cornish weather is so dreary
Another shower in the air
Rain and awful bleary
Make us give up in despair.

Cornish weather is boring,
New-cut hay on the ground
Gives no early warning
Rain clouds all around.

Cornish weather is eerie
Sunshine in a shower
As the rain pours down
Almost every hour.

Cornish weather gives a soaking
Washing lines are a waste of time.
Believe me I'm not joking,
'Cause the clothes get wet a second time.

Cornish weather is safely-safety
A snow blizzard is rare
Snug and ice-free as a baby
'Cause the rain won't let it dare.

R Rapson

THE FALLOW FIELD

With powerful stride, the farmer goes
Across the field where barley blows.
Through the copse, to the fallow field
One more year without a yield.

Three years running, he'd planned a crop
But three years running his plans he'd dropped.
The soil was shallow, thin and poor,
Other fields, with grace gave more.

Rest it may and yield no more
Till strength and goodness time restore.
Perhaps the farmer, strong and blithe
Should heed its pattern, shape his life,
Should sometimes let his striving lie
Fallow and let the race go by . . .
Till refreshed and reborn, his spirit may find
That nature's example is good for mankind.

The farmer knows his mortal span
Is brief within the Immortal plan.
Yet short or long though his service be
The Eternal Earth will always be.

Deirdre White

WAS IT ONLY A RAINDROP

Why did the raindrop come down from the sky?
Did it fall? Overflow?
Was it sent with a mission?

Was the raindrop reluctant
to leave where it was
happily sailing as part of a cloud?

Was the raindrop unconscious
of all that transpired
on the dry and drying crust of the earth?

Or was the raindrop waiting the moment,
ready and willing to give up its life
to be life-giving drink for the thirsty land?

Whatever the reason, it came in profusion,
one drop not enough, it poured and poured,
wherever it landed the earth was transformed:

Barren ground burst forth in profusion of growth
colour and perfume became its response
and the trees were laden with fruit.

Oonagh Twomey

EASTER MEANS MORE THAN EGGS

When some people think of Easter, they think of chocolate eggs,
Wrapped in coloured packages, displayed along the shelves.
Others think of springtime, when flowers begin to bloom.
But Christians think of Jesus - risen from the tomb.

Eggs will soon be eaten, the shelves will soon be bare.
The flowers will fade and wither - no longer sweet and fair.
But still the Easter message that Jesus lives again.
Remains in hearts that love Him, giving glory to His Name.

So friend, if you don't know Him - the One who died for you.
This Easter could be special - make Him your Saviour too.
You will have a new beginning - just like the start of spring.
Give your heart at Easter to Christ our Risen King.

J Smyth

BARE ROCK

Bare rock
Unlikely place to hold new life.

High in the mountains
The spring sunshine
Explores the rocky crevices
With warm fingers of light.
Tiny-petalled flowers appear,
Lichens colour the grey surface,
A few thin blades of grass spear upwards.
In awe, we wonder
How such frail life-forms
Can come to birth
In such an arid landscape,
Where stormy winds
Could loose their fragile hold.

Bare rock
Unlikely place to hold new life.

Deep in the rock
A tomb hewn out
And in it laid
The body of God's Son,
Cruelly crucified
High on a wooden cross.
A mighty stone was rolled
Sealing Him in the grave
Until that Easter morn
He conquered death,
Came from His rocky tomb
Into the fresh spring air
Alive and risen glorified.

Bare rock
In spring can bring forth life.

Roma Davies

THE SPRING SAVIOUR . . .

The unrelenting grip of winter
shows no sign of abating
as the hard harsh climate
dulls and enslaves our minds
as we exist tied
to the chill dead land
of penetrating winds
ice, snow, rain and still more ice.

Then a new day dawned
as the creative vital essence
surged into the sleeping earth
flowing into dormant roots
like life engendering
blood streams
powering them to develop
and push through
the hard resistant soil.

Where they burst
out into beautiful blossoms
as the force of life
regenerates the warming world
and makes our spirits rise
as like the flowers in bloom
we live again on earth
while our souls join
in the sacred psalm
of everlasting spring.

Stephen Gyles

SPRING WILL BE A LITTLE LATE . . .

Patient in
The sheltered hollow.
Waiting for
The days to mellow.
Heavy budded
Pussy Willow.
Waits on
Better times tomorrow.

Spring lies low
While winter lingers.
Jack Frost nips
At tips of fingers.
Holds at bay
Those feathered singers.
Ripple breezes,
Bluebell ringers . . .

Donald Harris

SUMMER

Long hot sunny days,
Soaking up the powerful rays,
Sunburned bodies litter the beach,
Common sense has gone, out of reach,
Creams and lotions must now be applied,
To cool, and soothe, anything is tried.

The smell of roses, as you sit in the shade.
Sipping your ice cold lemonade,
Cucumber sandwiches, wafer thin,
Strawberries and cream (just a small sin)
Lazy summer afternoons,
Enjoyed in this month of June.

July's garden fete's and school sports,
Trips to seaside resorts,
Making sand castles, out of reach
Of the sea as it creeps up the beach,
Summer fruits, ripe for picking,
No time for finger licking,
Some for the freezer, some for a cake,
Pies, puddings, jams, to make.

The earth is parched and dry,
The rain has passed us by,
A broken bottle, the sun's powerful rays,
Will soon set the fields ablaze.
So always take your rubbish home,
Save our fields, so we may roam.

Myrtle Elden

THE PLEASURES OF SPRING AND SUMMER

What to you are the first signs of spring,
Waiting for long dark days about to take wing.
Snowdrops and crocus through snow their heads peeping,
Awakened to life after dormantly sleeping?

Those spiky green leaves the soil pushing through,
Promise of lovely spring flowers to bloom anew,
Or stumbling around on unsteady feet,
New-born lambs with their plaintive bleat.

Songs of birds as their mates they follow
Will they again build in the old tree hollow?
On hedgerow bank, modest violets curl,
Trees overhead, buds waiting to unfurl.

Later, bluebell, primrose and wild aconite,
In a wooded glade, a glorious sight
With the warmth of sunshine and lengthening days,
One can be occupied in so many different ways.

Maybe watching rainbow after April shower,
A symbol to us of God's mighty power.
In summer, children's happy laughter playing in the sun,
The longer days with more scope for outdoor fun.

Walking country lanes and pastures green,
Absorbing all displayed on natures screen,
Beautiful sunsets with flaming dying ray,
Marking the close of a perfect summer's day.

Viewing mountain and waterfall, finding peace,
Watching endless tide, our tensions to release,
Summer holidays, picnics and days by the sea,
Lazing around with family, feeling happy and free.

Kathleen Jones

FOUR SEASONS

When the autumn leaves start
to fall, when the leaves start
to fall off the trees.

Then winter comes when it starts
to get cold. Everything is dead.
The trees are bare. Animal nature
makes everything dead.

Spring comes everything starts to
come back to life, nature brings
everything back to life.

The trees start to have leaves
Again the flowers start to blossom.

The birds start to sing a sign
that winter is finished.

Then summer comes when the sun is
shining and everything is bright and breezy.

Y Thompson

Seasons Of Reward

Each season of the year brings its own
regards, from deep, deep winter's days of sleep
and rest, that in turn will give way to early days
of spring, a promise of a future, still out of sight.
She holds a grip, firm in the beaut of the earth,
ready for the full glory of long summer days,
then once more, a return to quiet ways,
to have the time to reflect on winter's coming ways.

R P Scannell

BEING ALIVE

To walk by the seashore
Breathing the soft, salt air
Sand between my toes
The sea softly washing over my feet.

To move slowly through a meadow
Myriad wild flowers and tall grasses
Spreading a magical carpet
Of beautiful colour before me.

To simply sit and watch life
The happy passing scene
People of all ages
Occupied with their daily tasks.

To be here, just to be
Part of the vastness of humanity
A tiny speck in the universe
Being here, being free, being alive!

Barbara Manning

THE JOYS OF SPRING

When the wintry squall
Departs the northern shore
Then does a young man's fancy
Tickle him once more
For it is the season
When trampolines are fixed
Within the gym and on the grass
As the joys of spring bewitch.

Stuart Delvin

FROST

A night for magic!

> The moon,
> heaven-hung in velvet vastness
> silver-sprinkling-star-studded-
> shot the world with wonder,
> and shadows crouched like beasts
> about to spring.
> Silhouettes of trees -
> dark against darkness.
> Levelled lawn and limpid lake,
> bordered bush-black.

Singing silence,
like a spell of enchantment,
threaded thought with wonder.

> Unseen, unheard, he wrought his magic:
> breathing upon windows,
> touching trees with twisting fingers
> (leaves shrinking from his cold caress.)
> Slinking through grasses,
> sprinkling them with silver dust;
> threading slyly though still waters,
> leaving them stiff and numb with horror.

But with the morning light,
reluctantly acceding to the sun,
withdrawing into shadows, there to wait
for yet another night.

Josephine Haden

EXUBERANT MEADOWS

Bloom graceful, flowers across the land,
I think your loving splendour was planned,
So full of colour, to cherish the morn,
Of springtime's sunny, and caressing dawn,
We relish such blossom, each new born day,
And feel so honoured, and content, and gay.

Oak trees tall, and joyfully green,
the best of nature ever seen,
Heaven sent your seeds of beauty galore,
For people on earth, to love evermore.
Once full, then bare, as autumn comes nigh,
Such euphoria abounds, under a tender sky.

Green field so new, with flowing grass,
Sends rapture to heart and joy alas,
To see young rabbits run through your stem,
With cows at graze, is such a gem,
You feed them now, and for evermore,
Your blessing sent from Heaven's door.

Flow stream of crystal clear water now,
Through valley and glen, who ever bow,
Such clear and pure, and flowing tide,
Send forth your cleansing liquid wide,
To cleanse the heart of man, and beast,
Sent by God, I know at least.

Steve Kettlewell

MARCH OF THE SEASONS

The wedding of Earth and Heavens
procreates green-filled gardens,
beneath the moon Mother Earth
bursts with mystical rebirth
to awake the dormant power
that out of soil lures the flower.
Buried seeds take budding flight,
struggle gladly for the light
freely ebb and wisely flow
in a dream-bewitched meadow.

Night lit by the harvest moon,
red jays sing a serene tune;
mature nature spreads perfume,
all of living in full bloom -
roses smile at butterflies,
birthing stars invade the skies,
you and I embrace in trance
(lovers in nocturnal dance);
coral songs of cardinals start,
sparkling firelight in my heart;
humming poetry, I soar
o'er summer fields, unbound once more.

Twisting, dancing in the air,
falling leaves are everywhere;
sown on winds like scattered hopes
gather in each vale copse.
How like little fays and sprites
they pop and sail from left and right
filled with crunchy, scratchy joy!
Yellow-tinged, they flutter, coy,
winking fireflies, toward the ground
fiery carpets live with sound.

Through the white-capped trees I see
icicles apprising me
with cold eyes and withering dreams,
frozen light from ponds and streams,
mirroring the steel-grey skies
dots the wood with heavy sighs.
And glares of rotating wings
drifting fears flow of life's stings -
far above, a lone star twinkles
o'er winter hoar and snow-drift wrinkles.

Najwa Salam Brax

ANOTHER AUTUMN

Leaves are turning.
Fires are burning.
It's damp and cold with rain.
How sore the throat?
How thick the coat?
The year is on the wane.

'It's gone so fast!'
I hear you cry.
And sit with misted watering eye.
'Last New Year; when old 'Bill' came by,
Remember we had snow!'
I don't believe in looking back,
It takes too long you know.

Martin Buckley

IS IT SPRING?

Raindrops rattle on the windowpane,
Children playing in the lane,
Frightened by the lightning flash,
Come running home at thunder crash.

Wind slams door shut, with a bang.
Dustbin lid goes rattle clang.
Clouds in sky a dashing go,
Black, white and indigo.

We light the fire, brew the tea,
Huddle round the old TV.
Have to laugh at weather forecast,
That present sunshine will not last.

G W Bailey

THE SUMMER BREEZE

Warm summer wind, that whispering breeze,
Which moves the grass, my hair the trees
And sways them all, with unseen hand,
Like a conductor, with a silent band.

That whispering wind, which calls to me
And talks to every greenwood tree.
Its fresh air smell, the shimmering corn,
That greets us each and every dawn.

Long summer days, with night so short,
And showery storms, in which we're caught.
Those storms, which bring the fluttering breeze,
That twist and turn and bend the trees.

So here I'll stand, in awe and pride,
And on its wings, attempt to ride.
To savour this, to drink its wine,
Yet know, it will soon be wintertime.

When icy gusts will chill our veins,
And Jack Frost paint our windowpanes.
No leaves will adorn our sleeping trees,
So enjoy your summer, with its warming breeze.

R L Nettleton

WONDERS OF CREATION

With rainbow coloured wings here comes
The dragonfly, darting here and darting
There over fields and rivers nearby.
Perhaps you've seen one near a pond
Or maybe in your garden, this tiny
Creature is an asset to any person's garden.

It hovers here, and hovers there, as if
To be inspected, as if to say I'm beautiful
And not to be rejected.
Creation is so awe inspiring and not a man-made thing
But the glory and the honour goes to God Almighty,
Who created everything.

Pauline Potts

SAME AS YESTERDAY

The winter season's always the same
Closed the front door at seven am,
Hurry to work, same packed train,
Late on time, nose to the grind.
Nothing changes, start home again at five pm.
Same packed train,
Where does everyone abide all day?
Silent people sit, and look,
Heads buried in papers and books,
If you look their way
Too make matters worse,
Rain lashed down all day,
Same as yesterday,
Inside, one has a curse.
At the none stop city roar,
Must not moan, glad to get home,
Shut out the world, by shutting the door,
Turn on the gas fire
Pretend the warmth coming from crackling logs,
Warm one self in front of the fire,
Take off one's wet togs,
Sprawl in an easy chair,
With a cuppa
At last a moment too spare,
Unwind at the end of a trying day,
Put out one's mind
The thought
One's got to do the same tomorrow,
At seven am,
The very thought of it?

B G Clarke

TIDES OF EMOTIONS

Who says thus; goodbye to love, farewell to peace,
the helpless loves with unrequited dreams;
vast and timeless, majestically buoyant; drifting in seas,
of tears and anguish, indestructible themes.
The oceans too violent with heavy remorse;
twin currents of silence, but revealing the cause,
emotive chaos, with stormy guilt, lie deepening, shipwrecked at source!
But directed and channelled, suppressed from delight;
Crying in darkness, hopeless souls rendered to misery.
Bereft of compassion; the forces direct, producing monotony,
                                        no glimmer of light.
Drudgery like ennui, becomes the norm, a conscious
                                  outrage delaying the morn.
Monstrous wretch, impossibly vain, relies on
                            conditioning to hammer the pest,
inducing the babies was worth the expense,
generations of servants, believing the best.
To belief and faith, read gullible and blind;
to the tides of reason, rationale to find!
The sense is the power, logic the key, opens the door of blindness!
To find and to see.

C Thornton

WINTER'S REPROACH

January's pinching frost feels sharp
Against her exposed existence.
She wants him to hold her,
To shatter the unbearable silence
By saying something, anything,
It isn't import just as long as
He mentions her name,

Moments not shared have dissolved
Like a snowman in the deluge of time.
She's jeopardising her future hoping
That one last ray of hope will
Melt her untold misgivings away.

Vicky Stevens

A SEA OF BLUE

Away away to the bluebell wood,
Over 'yon distant hill,
In through woods, walk mossy ground,
Hear the skylarks shrill,
Garlands of lichen hang like lace,
I push my way on through,
A sea of blue assaults my eyes,
What a sight to view,
Bonny bluebells everywhere,
An aromatic smell,
Down the bank clear water springs,
From a shallow crystal well,
I'm away away to the bluebell woods,
Sweet solitude lies there,
Imagine you are here with me,
This moment we can share.

W Curran

SPRING HAS ARRIVED

Spring's putting on her best dress,
The birds are making their nests,
Winter has finally gone,
And lambs are being born,
The blossom is starting to grow,
Spring flowers are making a show,
Snowdrops and crocuses came first,
Primroses and daffs are about to burst.
They will be golden and bright,
Oh what a welcome sight.

A Cooper

ON PASSING A WOOD IN WEST YORKSHIRE

I passed a wood in early May,
In fresh green leaves and bluebells deep,
The summer young had still to age,
The bluebells stood as proof of this.

I do not think that I have seen
So many bluebells under trees,
If time could only freeze that place,
Preserve it for the human race.

And yet a silly thought is this,
The days will pass on into weeks,
The bluebells soon will fade away,
As daffodils died after spring.

It is the way for us the same,
The very year sounds out the knell,
There is a time for birth and growth,
A time to live, a time to die.

We should by nature see our years,
As little different than the dryad's,
Our centred lives would selfless be,
If we considered on the flowers.

For I passed a wood in early May,
In fresh green leaves and bluebells deep,
The summer young had still to age,
The bluebells stood as proof of this.

Robert Lockett

THE HOUNDS OF SPRING

Today, the lion sleeps, the couchant mass
Of Arthur's Seat, supine in freezing fog,
Deathlike, inert, in deepest hibernation,

Its gorse-broom mane hung stiff with rime. The grass
Scrunches beneath my boots in Hunter's Bog
And, white-on-black, the snow, in stark striation,

Anatomises Samson's Ribs, the Gutted
Haddie and the Crags, creating x-rays,
Conjuring up the granite outcrop's inner

Core. Beneath its sloping haunch, frustrated
Wildfowl, welded by webbing to Dunsapie Loch, graze
Fitfully on glass, or stand like sentinels, awaiting dinner.

The cauterising cold and battening wind
Drill boreholes in my face, whipping away
Involuntary tears, as in a centrifuge,

Anaesthetising cheeks and chin. Half-blind,
Bowed down against the tattooing hail, whose sharp artillery
Pierces and flays, upwards I climb. The huge,

Recumbent creature stirs, blinking its eyes,
Inclines its brow in greeting. Then, magically,
The mist evaporates, the stormcloud clears,

As in a miracle, the wan and watery light transmogrifies
Into tomorrow's sun. Castled and crowned, the city
Now in glittering panoply appears,

Ancient, mosaic, between the foreshore and the encircling slopes
Of Calton, Blackford and the Pentland Hills,
Stretching towards the horizon, beyond Queensferry.

Equally suddenly, the monochrome kaleidoscopes
Into a breath of primroses, snowdrops, daffodils,
Crocuses, catkin buds and flowering cherry.

Norman Bissett

SERENADING THE MOON

Sultry he sits as a solitary soul,
Strumming sweet tunes of Africa,
While serenading his golden moon.

Shut off from his daytime world,
Of hot and tepid - summery haze.
Relaxed in the cooling twilight,
While serenading his golden moon.

Ignores all else that occurs,
As with infatuated eyes he stares,
While serenading his golden moon.

Gary J Finlay

BLUE WHITE AND PINK

Clear blue sky, sun just coming up
Cloud's tinged with pink
At the start of the day
What a magnificent, September the first.

A cloud in the sky, just like a flame
Adorning the sky set off in blue
Waves of a flame, colour pure white
Lighting up the sky, this September morn.

Fluffy cloud that billows and bubbles
Some look like scales, touched in with blue
Vapour trails of planes, long gone away
Do you see that cloud, it's just like a tortoise.

You could not buy, the beauty you see
One gift that's free, in your busy day
Just stop, look round see what you see
A day that is perfect, for you and for me.

Carole A Cleverdon

THOUGHTS FLY TO SUMMER

Where are the summer days
Gone who knows where
Now winter days
We are going nowhere
Huddled and muffled
Against colder winds
Thinking of warm summer days
Where we dream
Holidays countryside
Takes on a glow
Sunshiny days
As all of us know
Bringing such pleasure
To each of our days
Then seasons change
To sad wetter days
Hoping it doesn't last long
For it seems
Thoughts fly to summer
And warm wondrous dreams.

Jeanette Gaffney

CLIMBING TREE (HAYES, KENT)

In yonder woods, quite close to me,
there is a lovely climbing tree
with boughs outstretched-like arms to hold,
the timid child - as well as bold.

Children's voices loud and shrill
excited with their new found skill
clamber through the branches high
to be the first to reach the sky.
Other children hang around
on lower branches near to the ground.

You are our special climbing tree
that grows in woods quite close to me.
Oh lovely, oak - if you could tell
of those who climbed and those who fell.

Time flies by and so,
children come and children go
but still - when all is said and done,
I think they will recall the fun,
of climbing up the lovely tree,
that stands in woods - quite close to me.

Jean Eyre

SPRING

Spring will be on its way very soon we know
We can tell by things happening we know
Winter is going, we put up with it,
We know even if it's heavy rain or even snow.

But spring can really bring much joy
To either a girl or a boy
We think of the flowers holding their heads
In lots of our lovely flower beds.

Then in spring in the country we walk
And see lovely flowers which makes us talk
The violets, primroses are starting to bloom
Which will bring joy to many very soon.

The nights will be getting shorter anyway
That gives lots of us joy any day
Soon we will be able to go for walks in the park
Even before it starts to get dark.

Then in our garden bloom is fruit trees, we will see soon
The apple and pear trees will soon be in bloom,
Though it's a long time for fruit to ripen anyway
We know summer will be here one day.

When spring has come and gone away
We think of summer most every day
The days are warm and give much pleasure
We can sit in the garden in our leisure.

We can pick fruit from our trees most days
And make jams and tarts anyway,
It really gives us much delight,
To know we can do things in the light.

Then autumn comes one more take care,
It's certainly colder everywhere
The leaves are falling off the trees
And it isn't just a breeze.

Then autumn makes us think winter isn't far away
We can't do anything about it anyway
But the four seasons give us joy
Even if we are a girl or boy.

K Taylor

ESCAPE

Better than all the rest they say
The ones you catch that get away
I guess I know just what that means
When I look at you in those tight blue jeans.

Your music echoes all my wishes
As I gaze into your tank of fishes
In the home with your creative touch
With the gorgeous dog you love so much.

In harmony we sing a song
It lifts us up where we belong
Moments in time meant to be
Remembered for eternity.

The morning mist is in the air
Two souls and a dog alone out there
I am laughing all the while
You carry me 'Macho style.'

We're nearly home the hour is four
My arms around your neck once more
The tender touch of your fingertips
Caressing the curve of my hips.

Your muscle tone and body contour
Moulding mine and saying 'I want her!'

Oh kiss me once before daybreak
When from this dream I'll be awake.

I knew you boy for just one day
And you're the one that got away.

Gloria Donaghey

THE BIRTH OF MY OWN ANGEL
(To Molly May my love)

I love the image of angels,
Painted drawn or penned.
But most of all their beauty,
Which seems to have no end.
But now I have no need,
To smile within a book.
For an angel came and kissed me,
And my heart and soul she took.

Marian Murphy

FRIENDSHIP

Water, flat, calm, smooth as the mirror's face,
Hills, now turning green, mixed yellow-browns,
We stand there dressed in black, our place, my place.
You, only understand my life's ups and downs,
You talk, I talk, we both stand and listen,
Where, friendships cuts through past recent pain,
The jigsaw piece of life that was missing,
God . . . it was good to see you again.

J S Liberkowski

FRIEND

Hand in hand
down country lanes,
fields of corn
and hedgerows bend.

Shining down
the sun so bright,
the love I feel
it feels so right.

I feel so proud
that you're my friend
to love and cherish
till the end.

Babs West

REUNION

Excited so much I don't know whether to laugh or cry
For I'm about to forget the time gone by
As if old friends reunited possessed the treasure of youth
Then anxiety strikes
Isn't it too late: all that is left of an old friendship -
faded postcards, black and white photos in a box in the loft?
One brings a controlled smile to this meeting
Knowing pride may have to pay the cost

Yes, to be expected, time has incurred her debts
Illusions tempered by disillusionment, the years taking their toll
Laughter came so easy then and to our friendship we gave our all
When no responsibilities weighed us down
We whiled away time as if she were ours to measure
And our fanciful schemes her treasure
The greying hair, the wrinkles make us look distorted
mirror images of our schoolgirl selves

If all the memories we recall are not enough to piece
together even one of those madcap schooldays.
The essence of what we were is invoked
Wafting down the years like a sweet familiar delicious scent
The honeysuckle bushes lining the path we followed to school
I take home the forbidden fruit
The giggling gangly gregarious schoolgirl
She chides me for being melancholy
Didn't we promise to follow the yellow brick road
and make reality of our dreams?
Yes, inside my mind I will go skipping along out of that
place back in time to a new becoming

Monica Gurney

A Christmas Wish

I wish every day
Could be Christmas
Children singing
Bells are ringing
People stopping
To say Merry Christmas
When night time falls
There's not a sound
To be heard
Children tucked
Up in their beds
Waiting for Father Christmas
To arrive.

Elizabeth Ann

LOVE AT FIRST SIGHT

I remember as though it were yesterday
when I saw you for the first time,
and my heart stood still, for I knew even then
that I wanted you to be mine.
But I never thought in my wildest dreams
that my hopes would ever come true,
though it's fair to say that the mood of each day
would depend on my seeing you.
And now as I look back over the years
and think what I've done with my life.
I know that for me the greatest joy
has come from being your wife.

Jacqueline Hartnett

THE FRIEZE

I feel the magic once again
It enfolds me
As I see the garden
Spread out before me.

I see the bridge
Broken now!
The ordered garden overgrown
With lavender and sage.

Broken paving hidden
By creeping plants
Gentians and wild strawberry
Growing in profusion.

The sun shining on
The hedgerows
Send a heavy scent
After the rain.

A path leads down
To the river
Under the weeping willows
Who dip their branches in the water.

The magic is there!
Everything stands still
A time frozen
Like a picture on the wall.

I know I will
Never see this moment again
But it's etched on my mind
And part of eternity.

Joan May Wills

ST ESTEPHE GARDEN

St Estephe Garden
Grape vines, peach and cherry trees
Calm tranquillity

Fig trees 'gainst barn wall
Hibiscus flowers waving
In afternoon breeze

Butterflies hover
Over buddleia bushes
Colourful picture.

Tamarisk boughs low
Lavatera blossoms pink
Graceful tall fir trees

Swallows swoop and dive
Chasing insects for their chicks
Hungry in barn nests.

Branches wave in breeze
Sunlight peeps through lacy trees
Birdsong all around

Somnolent trio
Lying under cherry tree
Azure sky above

St Estephe Garden
Escape from toil, stress and strife
Calm tranquillity.

Tonie Ritchie

SKIBBEREEN, CORK

Near the south west shore of Cork, by the Celtic Sea,
is a place called Skibbereen, where the spirit is free,
underneath the shadow of Mount Kid, on the River Ilen,
are Tragumna and Lough Hyne in this part of Ireland,
Mizen Head, Roaringwater Bay, Schull, and Ownahincha too,
little islands like: Rabbit, Hare, Horse, there are a few,
hear the legend of the lake monster of Lough Abisdealy,
to rival Scotland's Nessie, sometimes seen, unbelievably,
a mile from town are the remains of the Cistercian abbey,
maybe from the 14th century, or so they say, possibly,
and dating from 1826, there is a Grecian-style cathedral,
hereabouts are the Creagh Gardens, for you to see, an' all,
as we all say here in Skibbereen, to anyone from anywhere afar,
Cead failte romhat go dti an Sciobairin I gcroilar Chorcai Thiar.

Christopher Higgins

MEMORY LIKE THE IVY CLINGS

I close my eyes and wander,
Across the great divide,
I drift and hover slowly,
Until down to earth I glide.

I settle on a landscape,
White horse upon the hill,
How I loved that little village,
The memory lingers still.

I nursed up at the hospital,
Which closed long long ago,
I travelled with the ambulance,
On roads blocked up with snow.

I walked out with my sailor boy,
When he was home on leave,
But sadly down with ship he went,
And left us all to grieve.

So many years have passed since then,
I sometimes stop to ponder,
If we will ever meet again,
In the blue, blue, blue up yonder.

Anne McKimmie

THAT SPECIAL PLACE

It may seem strange to many
My special remembered place
It didn't have grand scenery
Nor holidays to thrill
But if I could go back in time
That's where I'd linger still

The little lane where the cherries grew
And the wild strawberries red
The chestnut trees with candles white
That bowed down overhead
Up that green aisle on a summer eve
I walked with the love of my life

The chestnut tree was our shelter
The sky our canopy
We needed nothing but our love
To make the hours complete
The love of my life and I

The happiest hours of my young life
Were spent 'neath that chestnut tree
We never longed for grand hotels
We were young, and in love, blissfully

That is my special remembered place
That little strawberry lane
And if I could turn back the clock
I would spend those hours again
With the love of my life
In that self same place
How I wish I was young again

Isobel Laffin

AROUND WIDDOP DAM

Sky above Widdop reflecting
the grasses browns, reds, greens
living water from dying growths
harnessed for life; it means

caught safely and piped for drinking
reaching body broken
until chains over - he can come
released; visits beckon.

Robert D Shooter

TO MY LOVE

Daffodils of new life
Daffodils of love
Waving from the cliff top
By our wild North Sea -
Oh they bring such memories
Such memories to me

Daffodils you gave me
Once so long ago -
Giving with them true love
There beside the sea -
Now they bring such memories
Such memories to me

Daffodils I gazed at
When alone in war -
Gathering from them courage
When I needed more
They were golden memories
Of what had gone before

Daffodils so precious
Seem to point the way
To a place called heaven -
Way beyond the sea
Where there'll be no memories -
    Only you and me.

Daphne Young

GRANDMA AND GRANPA'S COTTAGE

Grandma and Granpa's cottage
Solid and strong, it seemed
Its thatched roof came down to our shoulders
Inside the ceiling, all beamed
Outside a country garden
An orchard, dozing dogs
A washing line with dolly pegs
For winter - a pile of logs
Cats lazing in the sun
Granny doing her stitching
The smell of apple pie cooking
Coming from the kitchen
Granpa repairs a kitchen stool
Auntie Janet brings a tray of tea
Angel cake and crumpets
For my sister, my cousins and me
Our holiday haven
Curtains drawn for the night
Mum reading a bedtime tale
In the soft light
Day breaks and up we get
Boiled eggs and toast
Grandma and Granpa's cottage
The place we loved the most

Lyn Richard

THIS ENGLAND

From the misty spires of Oxford
To the calm of vales and dells
From the bustling streets of London
To the gentle coastal swells
This England is my homeland
From the frosty days of winter
To the summer blue skies clear
This England is my homeland
A place that I hold dear
The years I spent away
In foreign lands afar
Oh to be in England
The place that I hold dear
To see her white cliffs standing
Against the mighty foe
This England is my homeland
Wherever I may go
At last I stand here with her
This green and pleasant land
There is no other like her
This England my homeland

L E Davies

STAPEHILL GARDENS

The Abbey gardens, landscaped with care,
Lovely laid lawns of luscious green,
Beautiful colours are blended with flair,
Hundreds of flowers are here, to be seen.

Majestic trees stand tall and proud,
Red brick walls surround the ground,
Creeping ivy becomes their shroud,
Peace and quiet can always be found.

Shrubs and bushes sedately grow,
'tween rock pools and ponds.
Meandering waters casually flow,
shaded by, the many fronds.

A water fountain stands amid
the cottage garden neat and fair.
Sit and let your mind be rid
of troubles, stress and care.

The waterfall from rockery source,
flows on to feed the lake.
A peaceful end to a water course -
home to swan, duck and drake.

This tranquil place enjoyed by man,
ever changing with the season's sun.
Is this part of the Lord's great plan?
A glimpse of Heaven, for everyone.

Douglas Bishop

THE ABBEY

Most visitors go straight down to the river,
Flowing amongst green fields across its stony bed.
There on its banks, the families sit,
Paddling children skimming pebbles, daring the stepping stones.

He forks left amongst deserted grey stone ruins,
Into the roofless space where stood the chapel.
He sits as he has many times before, letting the silence speak.
This is a holy place, the atmosphere benign,
The centuries of prayer by black robed monks still linger here.
He noticed it when young, this peaceful sanctuary,
Returns to it in times of sadness, when friends and relatives depart.
He leaves it comforted, refreshed,
Part of his life which will be always precious.

Peter Hicks

WIDDECOMBE FAIR

It was a very special day we spent in glorious Devon.
We camped overnight on wild Dartmoor,
But woke thinking we were in Heaven.

The sun as it rose, turned the moor into gold,
The gorse and bracken gilding,
Wild ponies galloped by, birds started serenading.

But all too soon we were on our way,
After a cup of tea,
For the place to be was Widdecombe Fair
With so much there to see.

Cottagers displayed their crafts,
As did the small stall holders.
Tom Pearce trotted by on his old grey mare,
Huntsmen and hounds were bolder.

Children's sports were next on the scene,
As well as choir boys singing,
Men competed at felling trees,
Or by greasy poles were lingering.

Horses and dogs were not to be missed,
As well as a cattle show.
There was just some time for a Devon cream tea,
And then it was time to go.

So though today, I am old and grey
And have had lots of happy day,
I still remember that special one
And to Widdecombe Fair give praise.

Winifred Lund

SUBMISSIONS INVITED
SOMETHING FOR EVERYONE

POETRY NOW 2002 - Any subject,
any style, any time.

WOMENSWORDS 2002 - Strictly women,
have your say the female way!

STRONGWORDS 2002 - Warning!
Age restriction, must be between 16-24,
opinionated and have strong views.
(Not for the faint-hearted)

All poems no longer than 30 lines.
Always welcome! No fee!
Cash Prizes to be won!

Mark your envelope (eg *Poetry Now) 2002*
Send to:
Forward Press Ltd
Remus House, Coltsfoot Drive,
Peterborough, PE2 9JX

OVER £10,000 POETRY PRIZES
TO BE WON!

Judging will take place in October 2002